Cornerstones of Freedom

Powers of the Supreme Court

R. Conrad Stein

CHILDRENS PRESS®
CHICAGO

Library of Congress Cataloging-in-Publication Data

Stein, R. Conrad.
  The powers of the Supreme Court / by R. Conrad Stein.
    p. cm. – (Cornerstones of freedom)
  Originally published: The story of the powers of the
Supreme Court. 1989.
  Summary: A brief overview explaining how the Supreme
Court is the ultimate interpreter of our Constitution.
  ISBN 0-516-06697-8
  1. United States. Supreme Court—Juvenile literature.
2. Judicial power—United States—Juvenile literature.
[1. United States. Supreme Court. 2. Judicial power.]
I. Stein, R. Conrad. Story of the powers of the Supreme
Court. 1989 II. Title. III. Series.
KF8742.Z9S735 1995
347.73'26—dc20
[347.30735]   94-38266
                                                CIP
                                                AC

When the U.S. Constitution was written in 1787, it established a government in which power was split among three branches. The legislative branch is the Congress, which makes the laws. The executive branch is headed by the president and is responsible for carrying out the laws of the nation. The judicial branch, headed by the Supreme Court, is in charge of the federal court system. The Supreme Court acts as a referee and makes sure that all the laws and actions of government follow the principles laid down in the Constitution.

Originally, the number of justices who sat on the Court varied from six to ten. Beginning in 1869, however, the Court was composed of one chief justice and eight associate justices. This

The 1888 Supreme Court

format continues today. Opinions of the Supreme Court are decided by a majority vote. That majority is often as slim as five to four. The chief justice is considered to be the Court's leader, but he or she has only one vote.

More than five thousand cases a year reach the Supreme Court from the maze of federal, state, and local courts below it. If a party in a legal dispute is dissatisfied with a lower court's decision, he or she can appeal to a higher court. The case could reach the Supreme Court if it carries national importance, or if it challenges a law on constitutional grounds. Of the thousands of cases put before the Court, about two hundred are heard in a year. The Court must limit itself to focus only on the nation's most pressing problems.

The Supreme Court Building in Washington, D.C.

Every legal case is given a name based on the parties involved. If Mr. Jones sues Mr. Brown,

*A case is argued
before the 1867
Supreme Court.*

the case is called *Jones v. Brown*. If Mr. Jones
decides to sue the federal government, the case
might be called *Jones v. United States*. To most
lawyers, arguing a case before the Supreme
Court is the fulfillment of a lifetime dream.
Court hearings are not broadcast on television,
so the proceedings are surprisingly informal.
The justices will often interrupt lawyers by
asking questions during their arguments.

Decisions are made among the justices behind
closed doors. The justices who are on the
winning side of the vote are considered the
"majority," and those who vote on the losing
side are the "minority." As each case is decided,
one of the justices writes the formal opinion of
the majority. If a justice on the minority side

A restoration of the old Supreme Court chamber used throughout the 1800s. Since 1935, the nine justices have heard cases in a new building.

believes he or she has an important point to make, a minority opinion also will be written.

The writings of the Supreme Court justices soon become the classroom readings for law students across the country. The decisions are considered "precedents," which means that judges use Supreme Court decisions as the basis for future rulings. Since a justice's written opinion will be studied for generations to come, the justices write their decisions with painstaking care. Justice Louis Brandeis once rewrote a single opinion forty-three times! Some justices' writing is so cluttered with legal terms that an ordinary person could not understand it. Other justices will pour their souls into an opinion. On some occasions, an opinion is written so eloquently that the language enters our everyday vocabulary. The phrase, "Shouting *'Fire!'* in a crowded theater," came from the written decision of Justice Oliver Wendell Holmes, Jr. In his decision on a case involving the right to free speech, Holmes wrote, "The most stringent protection of free speech would not protect a man in falsely shouting *'Fire!'* in a theater and causing a panic."

Decision days at the Supreme Court are usually on Mondays. These can be occasions for emotional fireworks and high drama. Reporters crowd into the courtroom on the morning an important decision is to be announced. Everyone, including the justices, feels the excitement of a decision day. In 1954, the Court was to announce its decision in the school desegregation case *Brown v. Board of Education of Topeka*. It was such a momentous occasion that Justice Robert Jackson rose from his sickbed to be present in the chambers—he had suffered a severe heart attack just days earlier.

All Supreme Court justices are appointed by the president, with the approval of the Senate. The Senate Judiciary Committee holds hearings to interview the nominees. In the past, this process was just a formality. But in recent years, the committee has been harsh on Supreme Court nominees. The Senate rejected President Reagan's nominee, Robert Bork, in 1987. And in 1991, Clarence Thomas barely won the Senate's approval after he endured an embarrassing and painful approval process. In the midst of Thomas's hearings, a law professor named Anita Hill publicly accused him of sexually harassing her when she was his employee years earlier.

Supreme Court justices hold their seats on the Court until they die, or until they decide to retire. If a justice displays improper or corrupt behavior, the Senate can impeach and remove that justice from the Court. This has never happened in the Court's history.

Robert Bork, whose 1987 nomination to the Court was rejected by the Senate

The president often appoints people to the Court who share his political philosophy, but the president has no control over a justice's decisions. Every justice is charged with interpreting the Constitution objectively, and sometimes presidents are terribly disappointed with the decisions of the very justices they nominated. President Theodore Roosevelt appointed Oliver Wendell Holmes to the Court, but once Holmes was on the bench, he began making judgments that Roosevelt disagreed with. The president said of Holmes, "That man has the backbone of a banana."

In 1953, President Dwight Eisenhower nominated Earl Warren to be chief justice. Warren was expected to mirror the Republican

President Theodore Roosevelt (left) was not always happy with the decisions of his appointee, Associate Justice Oliver Wendell Holmes (right).

president's political views. But Earl Warren turned out to be an extremely liberal justice. He was the guiding force behind several civil rights cases in the 1950s and '60s. In some areas of the country, Warren was so disliked that billboards appeared on highways blaring out the message: IMPEACH EARL WARREN.

The most important responsibility of the Supreme Court is to keep alive the United States Constitution. The Constitution is often called a "living document" because of the way it has grown with changing times. The Constitution was written by men of the 1700s, and they could not possibly have imagined the conditions of

Chief Justice Earl Warren (left) confers with President Dwight Eisenhower (right) in 1952. Warren was such a controversial justice that many Americans wanted him removed from the Court (above).

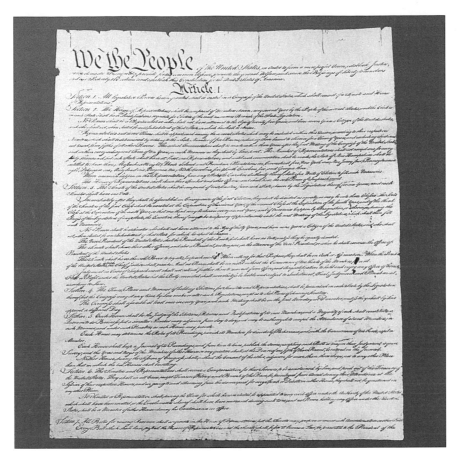

The U.S. Constitution, written in 1787, still provides the framework for our nation's laws.

20th-century life. For instance, electricity, automobiles, telephones, computers, and modern medicine did not exist in 1787. These inventions bring new and difficult twists to constitutional law. For instance, modern doctors have the ability to perform abortions, and to keep patients alive on artificial life support. These practices have forced our society to reevaluate the questions: when does a human life begin, and when does it end? The Supreme Court has taken on the responsibility of answering those questions as they relate to each individual's constitutional right to life.

So, the Supreme Court now must interpret the philosophy expressed in the Constitution in light of modern times. And at the same time, the Court must not actually *make* laws—that is the responsibility of Congress. The Supreme Court does, however, have the power to *overturn* laws or acts of Congress if they appear to be unconstitutional.

President James Madison

The Court did not always hold such power in American government. As defined in the Constitution, the Supreme Court was given far less power than Congress and the president. But the role of the Court changed dramatically in 1803 with a decision written by Chief Justice John Marshall. Marshall is today considered the master builder of the Court. He grew up poor and was largely self-educated, but he developed a brilliant legal mind. In 1803, Marshall heard arguments in a dispute between William Marbury and future president James Madison. What seemed to be a mild squabble between politicians, however, became the most important case in American history. In *Marbury v. Madison*, the Supreme Court for the first time overturned an act of Congress on the grounds that the act violated the Constitution.

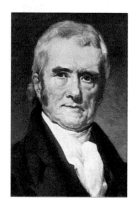

Chief Justice John Marshall

Writing his opinion in *Marbury v. Madison*, Marshall argued that the Court had the right to interpret the wording of the Constitution. The chief justice wrote, "If the laws conflict with

each other, the courts must decide on the operation of each." This ability to examine acts of Congress is called "judicial review."

Under Chief Justice John Marshall, the Supreme Court became a body that consistently made history with its landmark decisions. After Marshall's death, President Andrew Jackson named Roger Taney to be chief justice of the Supreme Court. Although Taney was an outstanding chief justice, history will always remember him for the 1857 case *Dred Scott v. Sandford*, perhaps the most disastrous decision ever handed down by the Supreme Court.

The House of Representatives (above) and the Senate make the laws of the land, and the Supreme Court must ensure that those laws are constitutional.

Dred Scott was a Missouri slave who lived
with his master for a brief period in Illinois and
the Wisconsin Territory. Upon returning home,
Scott went to court to obtain his freedom. He
argued that he should have been set free once
he left the slave state of Missouri and entered
Illinois and the Wisconsin Territory, where
slavery was forbidden. Dred Scott's lawsuit went
to the Supreme Court, where Taney and other
justices made two fateful declarations. First, the
Court ruled that since Dred Scott was a slave,
he was "property." Since he was seen as

Roger Taney, who was chief justice of the 1857 Court that made the infamous ruling in Dred Scott v. Sandford. *That ruling caused decades of hardship for African Americans.*

property, he was not an American citizen, so he was not allowed to take his case to court. Second, the Court claimed that Congress had no right to prohibit slavery in the Wisconsin Territory because it was not a state.

The Dred Scott decision outraged many people in the North who were opposed to slavery. The case is believed to be one of the major causes of the American Civil War (1861-65). A happier ending to the drama greeted the slave Dred Scott. Two months after the Supreme Court decision, Scott was given his freedom by a new owner.

Another Supreme Court decision that had disastrous effects on the civil rights of black Americans was *Plessy v. Ferguson* in 1896. In the 1870s, whites in the South began passing laws that prohibited blacks from voting in elections or attending schools with whites. Segregation laws forced blacks and whites to use separate seating areas on trains and in public buildings. In 1892, a black Louisiana man named Homer Plessy was arrested for sitting in a "white only" railroad car. Plessy argued in court that the segregation law was unconstitutional. Louisiana judge John H. Ferguson ruled against Plessy.

The 1896 Plessy v. Ferguson *ruling allowed segregation laws to continue for years. Even in the 1950s (right), African Americans were forced to use separate "colored" bathrooms, public schools, and public waiting rooms.*

So Plessy sued Judge Ferguson, and the case went to the Supreme Court, where it was heard in 1896. The Supreme Court ruled against Plessy, and for the next six decades, even more stringent segregation laws were passed in southern states. All of these harsh laws were seen as constitutional because of the precedent set by the Supreme Court in *Plessy v. Ferguson*.

The Supreme Court played a large role in the boom of big business in the late 1800s and early

A photograph of the 1896 Supreme Court, which ruled on the Plessy v. Ferguson *case*

For many years, young children performed dangerous manual labor in American factories.

1900s. Mining, automobile, and other massive industries were born and flourished in this period, and giant corporations grew wealthy. In case after case, the Supreme Court protected the rights of corporations to run their affairs without much government regulation. Even when Congress passed laws to end the practice of child labor, the Court struck down the laws, claiming they interfered with the conduct of business.

The nation's industries ground to a halt in the 1930s, when the Great Depression gripped the

Industries such as steel (bottom), oil (left), and locomotives (above) all grew rapidly during the Industrial Revolution of the late 1800s. Many huge companies grew to be extremely powerful monopolies. Some people thought monopolies were dangerous to the economy because they would not allow a free market to flourish. The Supreme Court of that era, however, allowed many industrial monopolies to expand and gain more power.

Hundreds wait in line for food in Times Square, New York, at the height of the Great Depression.

United States. One of every four workers lost his or her job, and previously well-off families were literally starving. President Franklin Delano Roosevelt and a Democratic Congress passed sweeping laws designed to provide relief for the poor. Roosevelt called his proposals "New Deal" economics. But a conservative Supreme Court rejected some of the measures. Roosevelt was so outraged that he tried to rebuild the Court with

his own appointees. Roosevelt supported a law that would increase the number of Supreme Court justices from nine to as many as fifteen. But this "court-packing" effort failed when Congress rejected the plan. As a result, the strength and independence of the nine-person Supreme Court grew.

Beginning in the 1950s, a long string of civil rights cases reached the Supreme Court. In the past, the Court's decisions had severely damaged the plight of minorities. But now the Court's civil rights decisions helped pave a better way of life for African Americans. Perhaps the single most important Supreme Court decision of the 20th century was *Brown v. Board of Education of Topeka* in 1954.

Justices of the 1937 Supreme Court (above). Many of President Franklin Roosevelt's (below) New Deal proposals were overturned by the Courts of the 1930s and '40s.

Linda Brown, the girl who was not allowed to attend an all-white school in Topeka, Kansas. Her father sued the Board of Education, and the case went to the Supreme Court.

In 1951, a railroad worker named Oliver Brown sued the city of Topeka, Kansas, because it would not allow his daughter to attend an all-white school in her neighborhood. When the case reached the Supreme Court in 1954, Chief Justice Earl Warren handed down a landmark decision condemning school segregation. Without a single negative vote, the Court overturned the older *Plessy v. Ferguson* decision. Earl Warren wrote, "In the field of public education the doctrine of 'separate but equal' has no place. Separate educational facilities are inherently unequal."

The *Brown v. Board of Education of Topeka* case was an instrumental step in the civil rights movement of the 1950s and '60s. It also was significant because Oliver Brown's lawyer was Thurgood Marshall. In 1967, Marshall became the first African American to sit on the Court when he was appointed by President Lyndon Johnson.

*Lawyers George
E. C. Hayes,
Thurgood Marshall,
and James M.
Nabrit (left to right)
stand in victory at
the Supreme Court
Building. They
successfully argued
the* Brown v. Board
of Education of
Topeka *case before
the Court. Thurgood
Marshall later
became the first
African American to
sit on the Court.*

SOME NOTABLE SUPREME COURT JUSTICES OF THE 20TH CENTURY

Louis Brandeis
(1856-1941)

Associate Justice:
1916-1939

Appointed by:
President
Woodrow Wilson

First Jewish
Supreme Court
justice

William O. Douglas
(1898-1980)

Associate Justice:
1939-1975

Appointed by:
President
Franklin Roosevelt

Served thirty-six
years, the longest
Supreme Court term
in history

Thurgood Marshall
(1908-1993)

Associate Justice:
1967-1991

Appointed by:
President
Lyndon Johnson

First African-
American Supreme
Court justice

Sandra Day
O'Connor
(1930-)

Associate Justice:
1981-

Appointed by:
President
Ronald Reagan

First woman
Supreme Court
justice

As the civil rights movement grew, Congress passed a sweeping civil rights act that outlawed racial segregation in public accommodations. In a 1964 case, the Supreme Court declared the new civil rights act constitutional, and forever buried the notion that separate-but-equal facilities were acceptable in the United States.

The 20th century has seen a distinct change in the role of the Supreme Court in our society. In its early years, the Court merely ruled on issues relating to the powers of the various levels of government. Today, however, the Supreme Court is the primary battleground for the most crucial and emotional issues in the United States. In

The Brown v. Board of Education *decision paved the way for school integration, allowing children of all races to attend public schools together.*

addition to laying the legal groundwork for the civil rights movement, in recent decades, the court has ruled on such issues as:

- Abortion—In 1973, the *Roe v. Wade* decision declared that states may not prohibit abortions within the first three months of pregnancy. This decision gave women the legal right to abortion in all states.

- Criminals' Rights—In the 1966 *Miranda v. Arizona* case, the Supreme Court ruled that suspected criminals must be informed of their rights when they are arrested. This means that police officers cannot force suspects to answer

Opponents in the abortion debate label themselves as "Pro-Choice" (in favor of abortion rights) or "Pro-Life" (against abortion rights); here, they confront each other on the steps of the Supreme Court.

questions if they do not have a lawyer present. Because of the *Miranda v. Arizona* decision, police officers must read the "Miranda rights" to everyone they arrest.

Advocates of prayer in public schools stage a protest in Washington, D.C.

• Separation of Church and State—The Constitution states that the government shall not restrict citizens' religious beliefs or practices. In the 1962 *Engel v. Vitale* case, the Supreme Court made it illegal for public schools to force students to recite prayers in school. The Court reasoned that since public schools are run by the government, it would be improper for the schools to promote a religion by conducting student prayers.

Another Court decision on this subject was 1984's *Lynch v. Donnelly*. The issue here was whether local governments have the right to display Nativity scenes at Christmastime. The Court ruled that a government's Christmas display does not mean that it is promoting a certain religion or excluding others. Therefore, local governments do have the constitutional right to display Nativity scenes.

A protester burns an American flag.

- Freedom of Speech—The
  Constitution gives people the
  right to free speech. But do
  people have the right to express
  themselves in ways that nearly
  everyone finds offensive? Does
  a person have the right to burn
  an American flag as part of a
  political protest? The 1989 *Texas
  v. Johnson* decision says that an
  individual's constitutional right
  to free speech allows him or her
  to burn an American flag.

*Some of the most
important decisions
in the United States
are made behind
the doors of the
Supreme Court's
chambers.*

Almost every decision by the
Supreme Court is hailed by some
Americans and cursed by others. Issues such as
abortion and flag burning touch off bitter
debates that spark emotional protests on the
steps of the Supreme Court Building. But the
justices of the Supreme Court try to shut out all
of this sound and fury so they can remain
objective. The nine justices must interpret the
Constitution, no matter what public opinion
polls might say. As Oliver Wendell Holmes once
said of the Court's position in American society,
"We are very quiet here, but it is the quiet of a
storm center."

GLOSSARY

abortion – a medical procedure that ends pregnancy by removing the fetus from the mother's womb

appeal – to bring a legal case to a higher court

argue – to present a case before a court or judge

chief justice – the head of the Supreme Court

constitutional – a law or act of Congress that follows the rules set forth in the Constitution

executive branch – the branch of government headed by the president

impeach – to formally accuse someone of a crime

Chief Justice Roger Taney

judicial branch – the branch of government that is headed by the Supreme Court

judicial review – the Supreme Court's ability to examine and overturn acts of Congress

landmark – an event of great significance

legislative branch – the branch of the government that consists of the Congress

overturn – to reverse, to declare illegal or unconstitutional; the Supreme Court can "overturn" laws of Congress or decisions of lower courts

precedent – a court ruling that forms the basis of future rulings on similar issues

segregation – the separation of races of people; for many years in the South, "segregation" laws forced blacks to use different public facilities than whites

sue – to take a person or institution to court seeking justice or financial rewards

unconstitutional – a law or act of Congress that goes against the principles set forth in the Constitution

segregation

TIMELINE

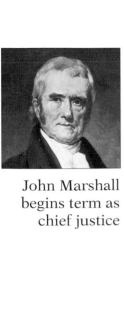

John Marshall
begins term as
chief justice

Dred Scott
v. Sandford
(civil rights)

Thurgood Marshall
joins Court

1787 United States Constitution signed
1789 Supreme Court first meets
1791 Bill of Rights ratified

1801
1803 *Marbury v. Madison* (judicial review)

1836 Roger B. Taney begins
term as chief justice

1857
1861 ⎫
1865 ⎭ American Civil War

Plessy v. Ferguson (civil rights) **1896**
Oliver Wendell Holmes joins Court **1902**

Louis Brandeis joins Court **1916**

The Great Depression begins **1929**

1933 ⎫
⎬ Franklin D. Roosevelt's presidency
1945 ⎭

1954 *Brown v. Board of Education* (civil rights)

1962 *Engel v. Vitale* (prayer in public schools)

1966 *Miranda v. Arizona* (criminals' rights)
1967

1973 *Roe v. Wade* (abortion)

1981 Sandra Day O'Connor joins Court

1989 *Texas v. Johnson* (freedom of speech)

1991 Clarence Thomas's nomination hearings

INDEX (*Boldface* page numbers indicate illustrations.)

PHOTO CREDITS

Cover, SuperStock, Inc.; 1, ©The National Geographic Society, courtesy, The Supreme Court Historical Society; 2, ©Cameramann International; 3, Bettmann; 4, SuperStock, Inc.; 5, North Wind Picture Archives; 6, Architect of the Capitol; 8, 9 (right), AP/Wide World; 9 (left), North Dakota Heritage Center, State Historical Society; 10 (left), UPI/Bettmann; 10 (bottom), UPI/Bettmann Newsphotos; 11, Photri; 12 (top), Library of Congress; 12 (bottom), Bettmann; 13, AP/Wide World; 14, 15, Bettmann Archive; 16, UPI/Bettmann; 17, Collection of the Supreme Court of the United States; 18, Bettmann Archive; 19 (all three photos), North Wind Picture Archives; 20, AP/Wide World; 21 (top), Collection of the Supreme Court of the United States; 21 (bottom), 22, 23, AP/Wide World; 24 (far left), Collection of the Supreme Court of the United States; 24 (left center), Bettmann Archive; 24 (right center), UPI/Bettmann; 24 (far right), Reuters/Bettmann; 25, SuperStock, Inc.; 26, AP/Wide World; 27, UPI/Bettmann; 28, AP/Wide World; 29, Photri; 30 (top), Bettmann Archive; 30 (bottom), UPI/Bettmann; 31 (all photos), Bettmann

ADDITIONAL PICTURE IDENTIFICATIONS

Cover: *The Supreme Court Building in Washington, D.C.*
Page 1: *The 1993 Supreme Court. Front row (left to right): Sandra Day O'Connor, Harry A. Blackmun, William H. Rehnquist (chief justice), John Paul Stevens, and Antonin Scalia. Back row (left to right): Clarence Thomas, Anthony M. Kennedy, David H. Souter, and Ruth Bader Ginsburg. In 1994, Harry Blackmun retired and was replaced by Stephen G. Breyer.*
Page 2: *Exterior of the Supreme Court Building.*

STAFF

Project Editor: Mark Friedman
Design and Electronic Composition: TJS Design
Photo Editor: Jan Izzo
Cornerstones of Freedom Logo: David Cunningham

ABOUT THE AUTHOR

R. Conrad Stein was born and grew up in Chicago. After serving in the U.S. Marine Corps, he attended the University of Illinois, where he earned a B.A. in history. He later studied in Mexico, where he received an advanced degree in fine arts.

Reading history is Mr. Stein's hobby. He tries to bring the excitement of history to his work. Mr. Stein has published many history books aimed at young readers. He lives in Chicago with his wife and their daughter, Janna.